Pie People

by Mark Stultz

illustrations by Heather Spalding

DORRANCE PUBLISHING CO
EST. 1920
PITTSBURGH, PENNSYLVANIA 15238

Dorrance Publishing Co
585 Alpha Drive
Suite 103
Pittsburgh, PA 15238
Visit our website at *www.dorrancebookstore.com*

ISBN: 978-1-6453-0287-2
eISBN: 978-1-6453-0886-7

To my wife, kids, and unique friends who inspire me every day with their talents, hearts, and desire to be true to themselves and embrace the journey vs. following the herd. Your pies are perfect.

~Mark

For my incredible family and friends, who have always supported me and given me wild ideas that I probably shouldn't try, but do. A special thanks goes to my Granny, who has kept me going all these years by inspiring me with her endless encouragement, strength, and determination.

~Heather

Pie People is a book with a simple thought process that can apply to everyone in the world, no matter what age. My hope is that it will serve as a tool to help you discover and share your unique gifts and talents, to encourage people to celebrate each other, and recognize that we are equals, no matter who we are, or where we live.

This is also a book of self-discovery, people celebration and people balance. I have included a simple workbook section where you can apply your personal inspiration and ideas.

This process will hopefully allow you, the participant, to take a few moments and say hello to self. You may also find that you can say hello to few pieces you have left behind or maybe are just beginning to see and use.

Please allow this experience to help you create your own recipe, that you may be fulfilled, happy, and discover your purpose.

Pie People

Enjoying pie is not always about making, baking, decorating, selling, or eating pie. Enjoyment even transcends discovering secret pie ingredients.

Enjoying pie is not always about cherry
pies, pizza pies, pumpkin pies, chocolate
pies, cookie pies, cobbler pies, or pie á la
mode.

What other types of pie are there?

Imagine that everyone in the entire world is created equally as pies! We are united by one theme, yet completely individual. We are Pie.

How can people be pie?

A pie can be both a food and a universal language. Everyone around the world can enjoy a delicious pie!

Pie People can be both language and symbol for who we are and who we can be as unique individuals.

We Pie People are all made up of eight pieces, and those eight pieces make up our unique gifts and abilities.

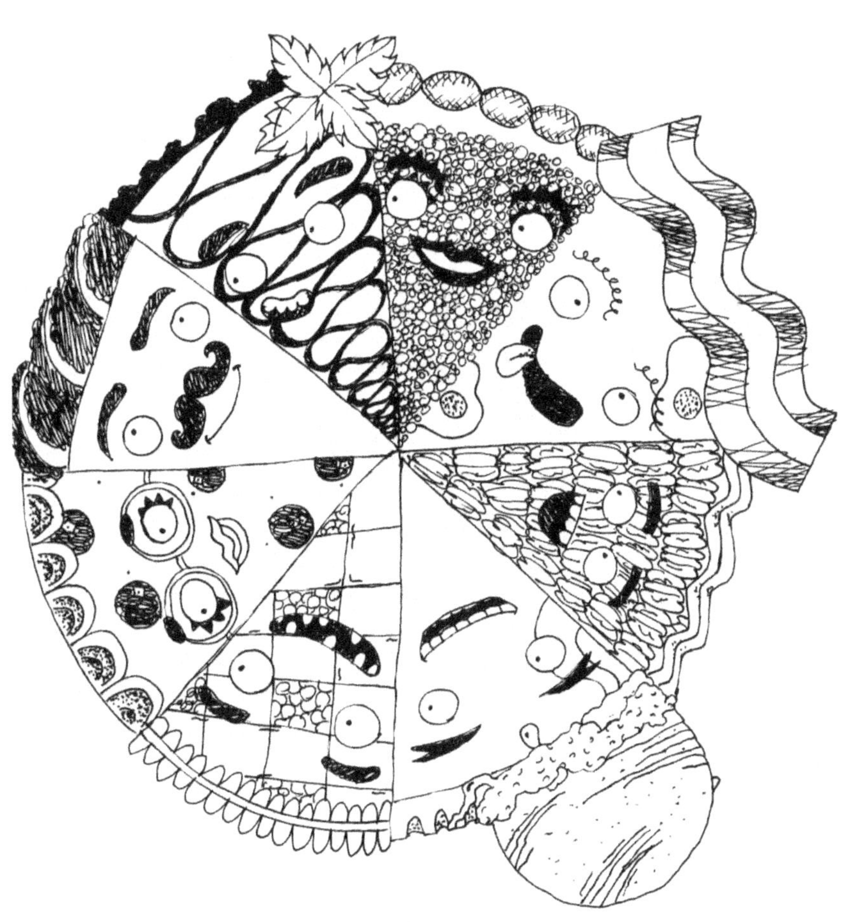

Everyone has different natural gifts and abilities that make up their unique combination.

Our gifts and abilities come from the creative, physical, spiritual, or intellectual parts of our natural being.

We all have them, just in different combinations and proportions.

What are these gifts and abilities?

Knowledge DANCE Teaching

Wisdom Writing Encouragement

Artistic Expression Singing Giving

Athleticism Prophecy Leadership

Music Service Mercy

Knowledge

Wisdom

Artistic Expression

Athleticism

Music

Dance

Writing

Singing

Prophecy

Service

Teaching

Encouragement

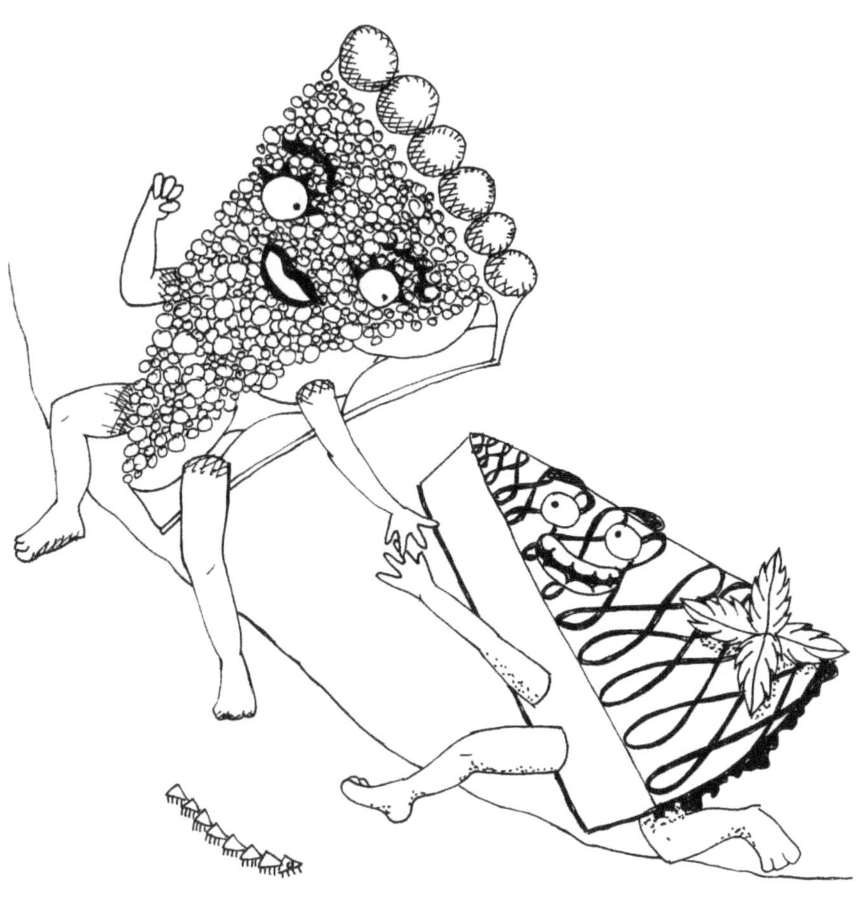

Giving

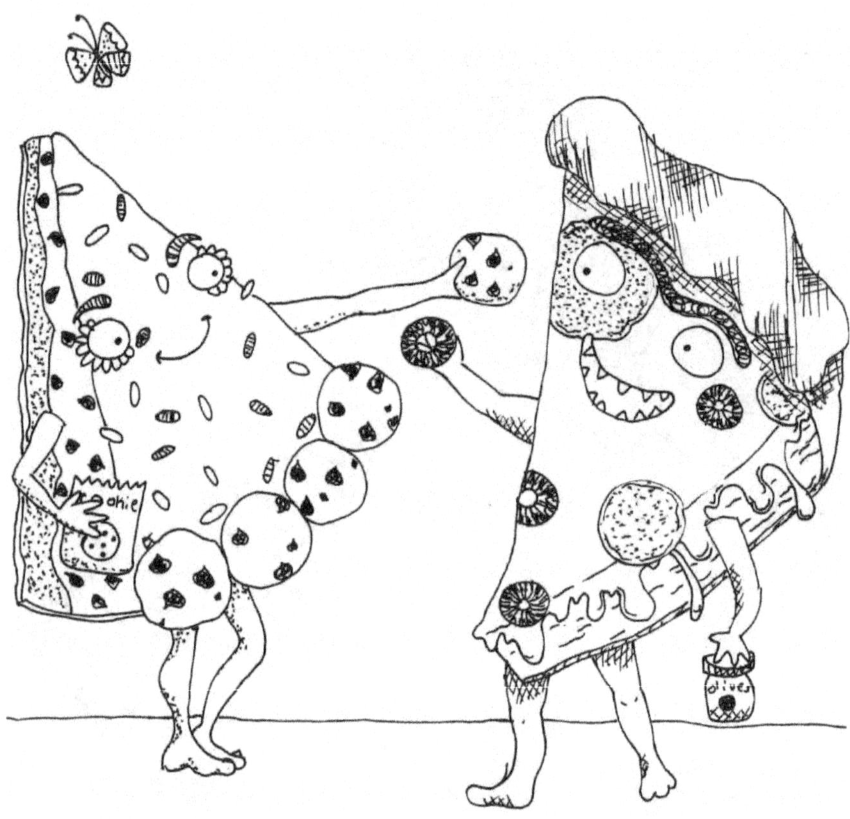

Leadership

Mercy

Some gifts and abilities may start out as a small idea, dream, or even just a feeling. However tiny they may be, they can be developed into pie pieces, too!

Most importantly, they all come from the natural, creative, or spiritual roots in our special and unique personalities..

Some of our gifts and abilities are easy to see, while others are more of a challenge.

There is no magic formula for understanding our pieces of gifts and abilities. They reveal themselves at the right time, when we are ready and listening.

32

As we already know, this big, beautiful world is full of millions of people who are all different and unique.

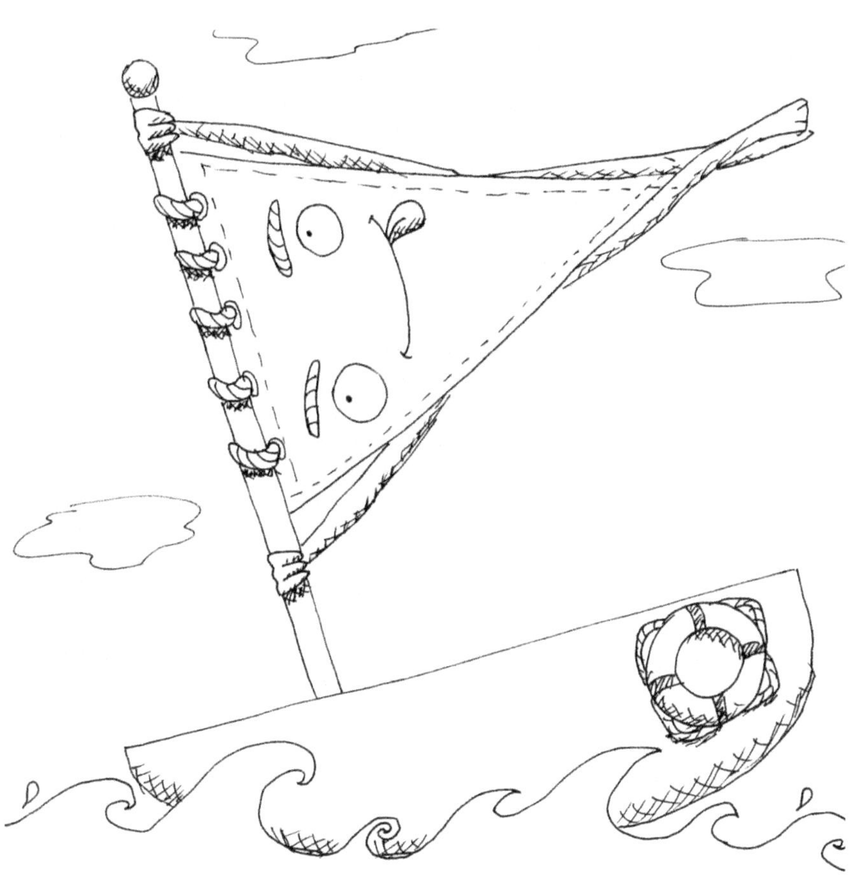

So, we are each completely different and completely equal. How can that be?

Being born to this earth is an amazing miracle in itself. Being alive, breathing, and able to explore who we are and why we are here is part of the beautiful journey of life, regardless of where we live in the world.

Why would one person, born as a precious baby full of love, not be equal to the newborn baby across the planet from a different family and culture?

We are born equal, and when our amazing journey is over, we die in equality, too. It does not matter who or where we are.

Think about how we are all created equal in gifts and abilities. Our eight pieces are not the material things of this earth.

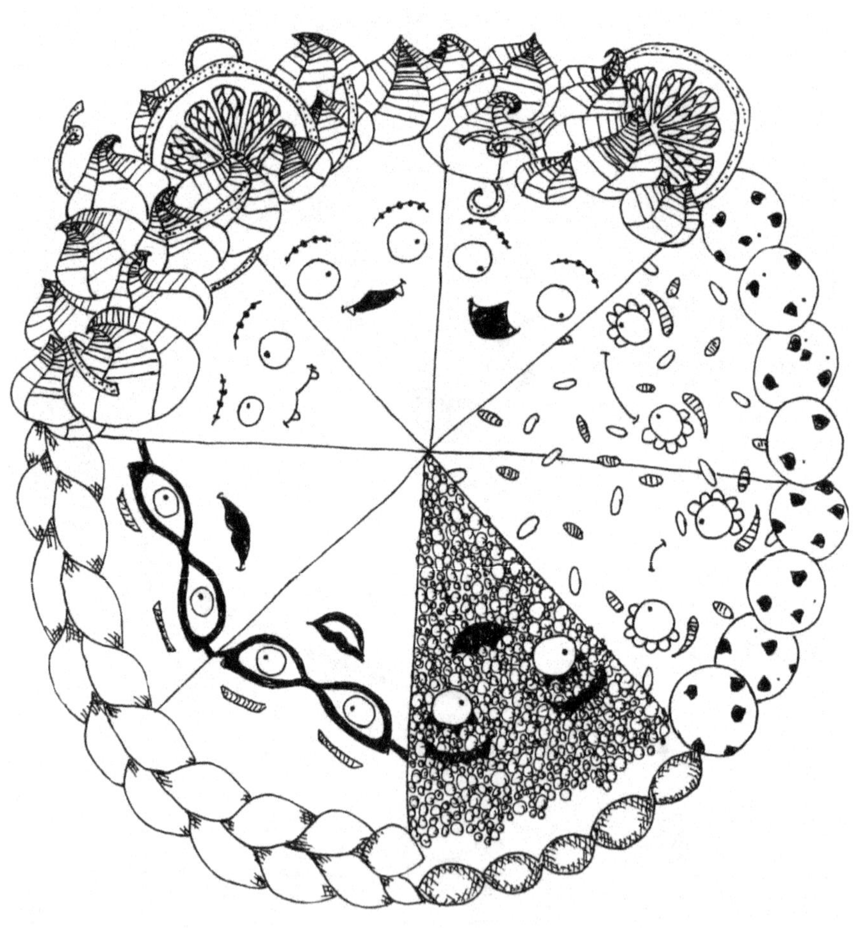

One of the most satisfying things a person can do is to realize their gifts, abilities, and purpose in life.

The other most satisfying thing a person can do is to share those gifts and abilities with their fellow Pie People!

The act of sharing our unique combinations and pieces with each other helps make the world exceptionally beautiful, perfect, and fascinating.

We are all born with our full potential inside, ready to be discovered.

Our goal in life is to find, unleash, and illuminate our pie pieces. Then we can share them with the world and help others find and share their pie pieces, too!

It does not matter what we do, how old we are, or where we live—our pies are all equally important. A vice president of a corporation, a cashier, a world-class athlete, a factory worker, and a musician are all equally wonderful and important!

The combined ingredients, pieces, gifts,
and abilities of Pie People fill our big world
with perfect balance.

Some people understand what their pie pieces are like early on in life; others spend more time looking within and around themselves to understand who they are and what they are made of.

Sometimes we can see natural gifts and abilities in other Pie People, even before we see it in ourselves. If you see a gift in someone around you, be sure to let them know and encourage them!

Some people are simply made up of two or three gifts and abilities, and these fill up all eight of their pie pieces. Others may have eight different pieces altogether.

If our pieces are our gifts and abilities,
what about our crust, topping, and pan?

Our crust, topping, and pan are our earthly self, what people see from the outside.

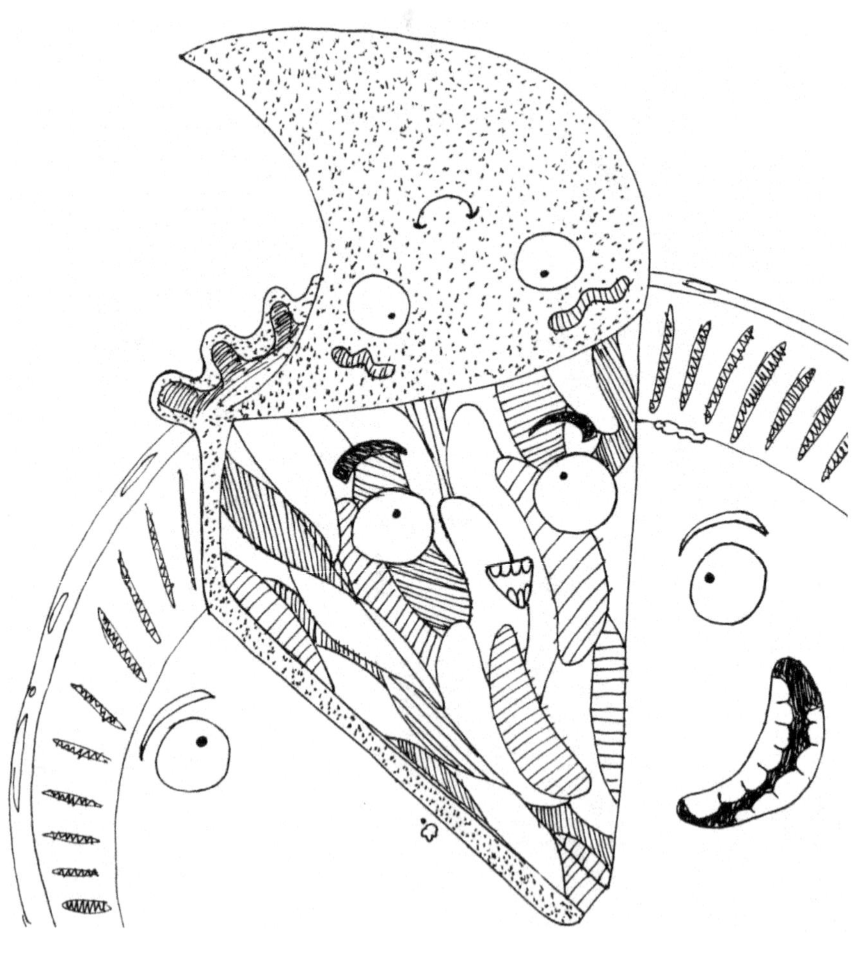

Our filling is our inner self, related to our gifts, abilities, pieces, spirit, heart, soul, mind, and character.

Our pan holds us together, and it allows us to travel and move around to be shared with others.

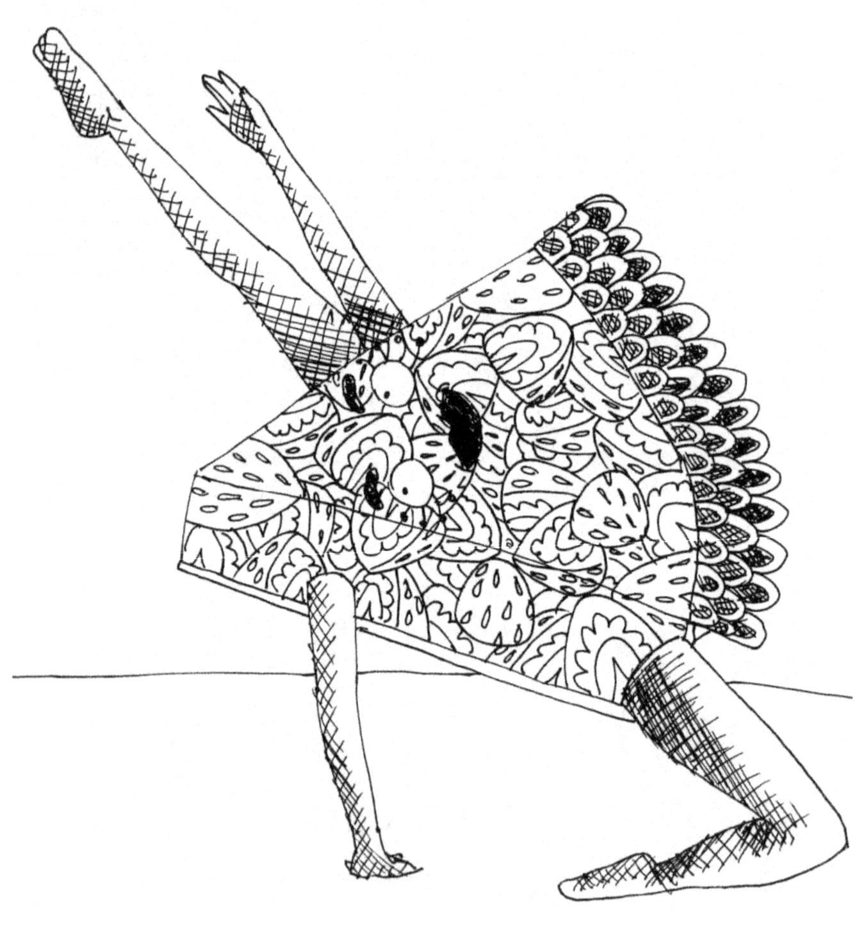

Our crust, pan, and filling need each other in order to be complete and functional. Without this balance, we are unable to live to the fullest.

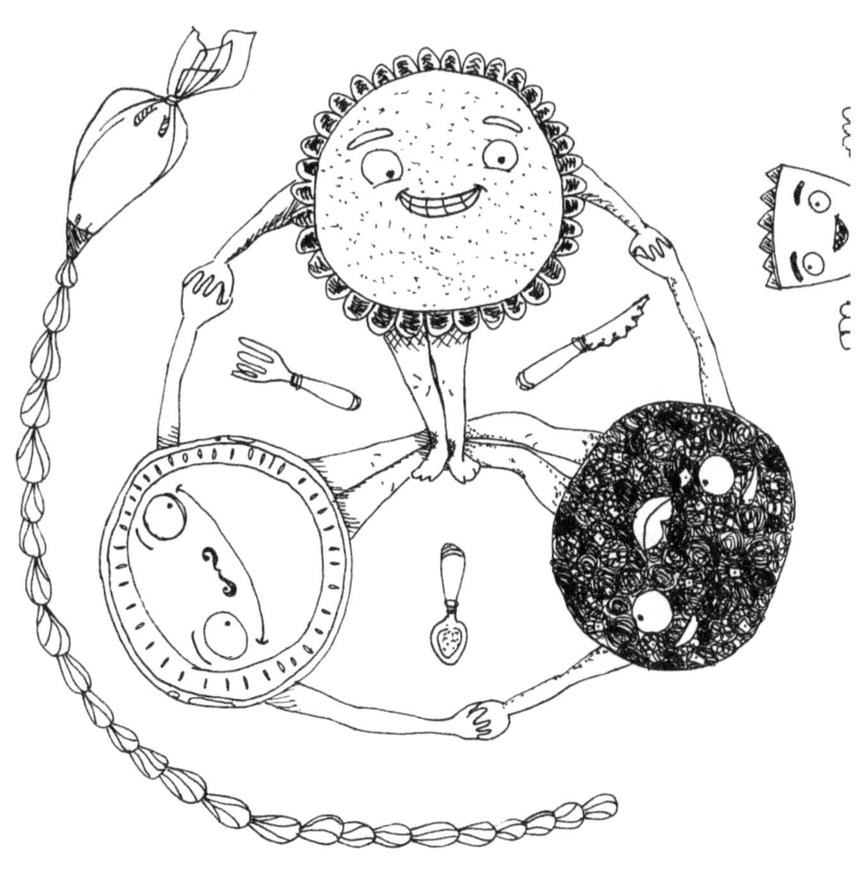

53

Our eight pieces, pan, topping, filling, and crust, all work together and are part of our uniquely personal combination.

Some pies have whipped cream, shiny sprinkles, or glaze, but underneath all that fancy topping there are still just eight pieces.

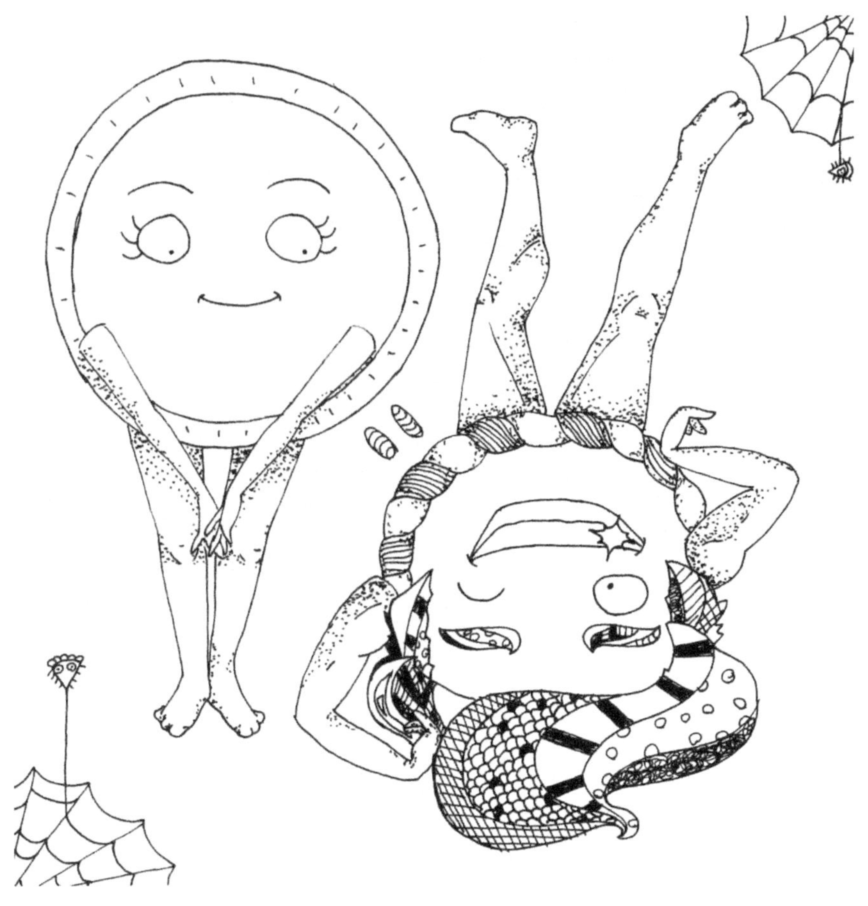

No matter how fancy looking our pie may be, it is still a pie.

A pie may be fancy, shiny, tall, sugary, glittery, fluffy, and colorful, but it is still a pie with just eight pieces, a crust, and a pan.

Now, let's look at our pie in a different way.

What if our pie wasn't just gifts and abilities, but was instead types of life focus?

Now, think about our pie pieces changing over our lifetime.

As our priorities in life change, our pie changes.

Now, let's look at our pie in another way.

What if our pie wasn't gifts and abilities,
or life focus, but a balance of love and fear?

All feelings and actions can be traced back to either love or fear.

What could that pie look like?

As newborn babies, we might have pies
just completely full of love!

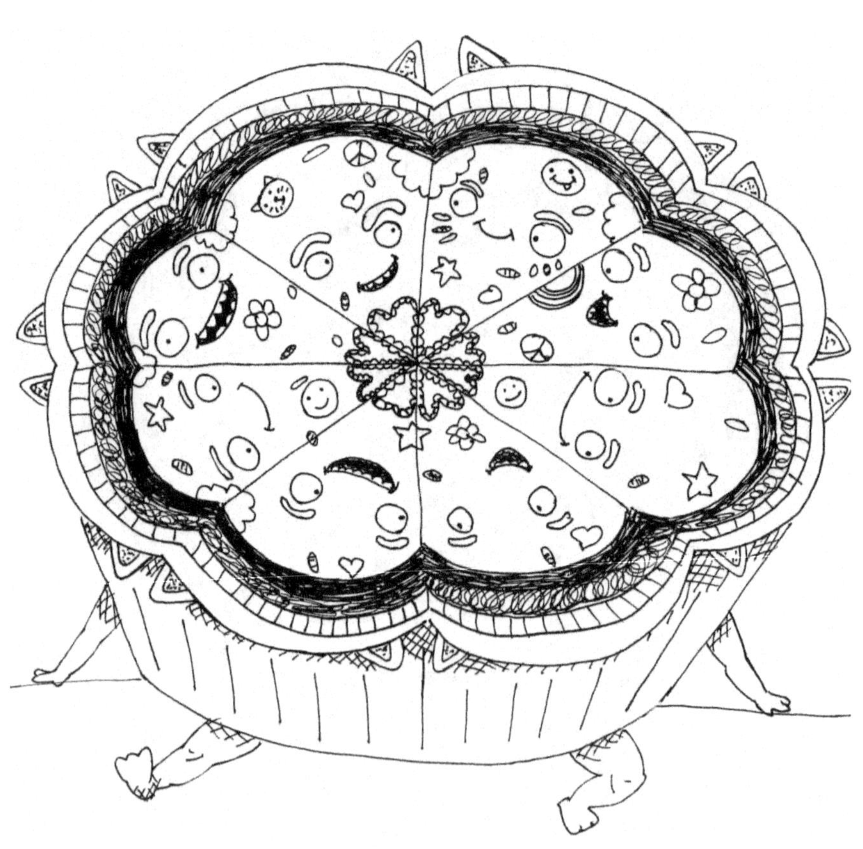

As we grow up, our pie may begin to include more fear pieces as we experience reality and responsibility firsthand until we find a way to manage fear and uncertainty.

When life comes full circle and we become older and wiser, our pie may once again reflect more of the love we have felt throughout our lifetime of memories.

A pie has a short life, just as we do, but the lasting flavor, happiness, and impact of a pie can last much longer than the actual life of a pie.

Let's make our pies to last, make our pies to be full of individuality, make our pies to be shared, and finally, make our pies to love and be loved!

What do your pie pieces look like?

Ask a friend if you don't know!

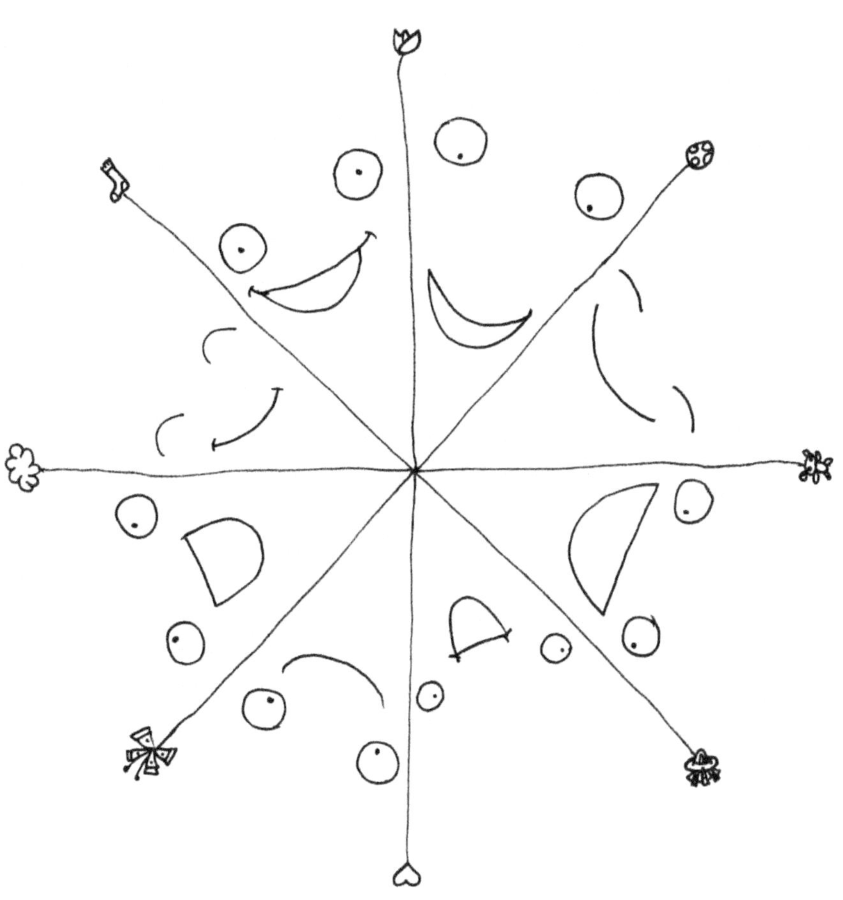

What would you like your pie pieces to look like?

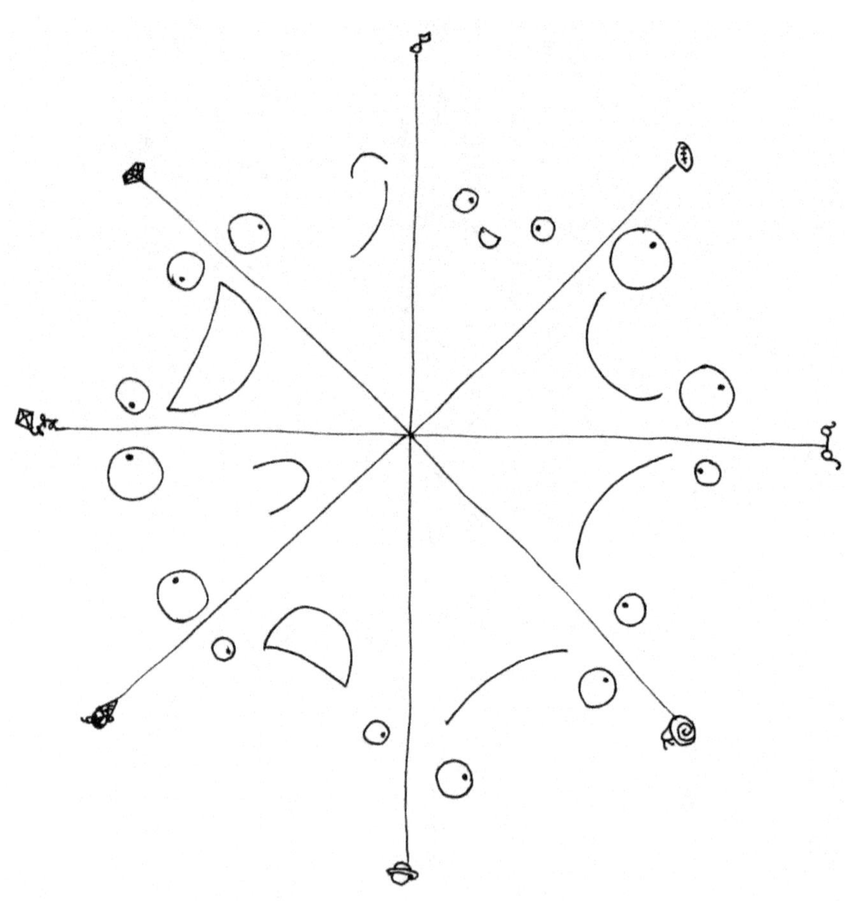

What would your best friend's pie pieces
look like?

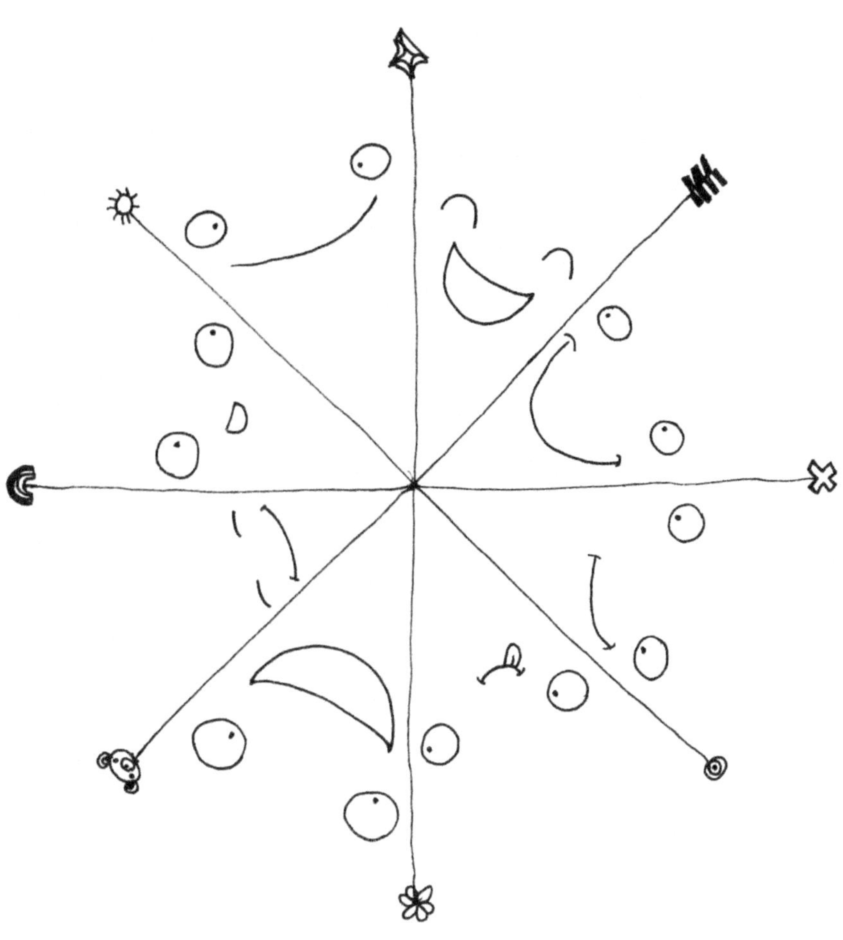

How much time do you spend in fear of people, things, or situations vs. loving people, things, or situations? How much of your day is spent thinking negatively about yourself or how much others may have hurt you?

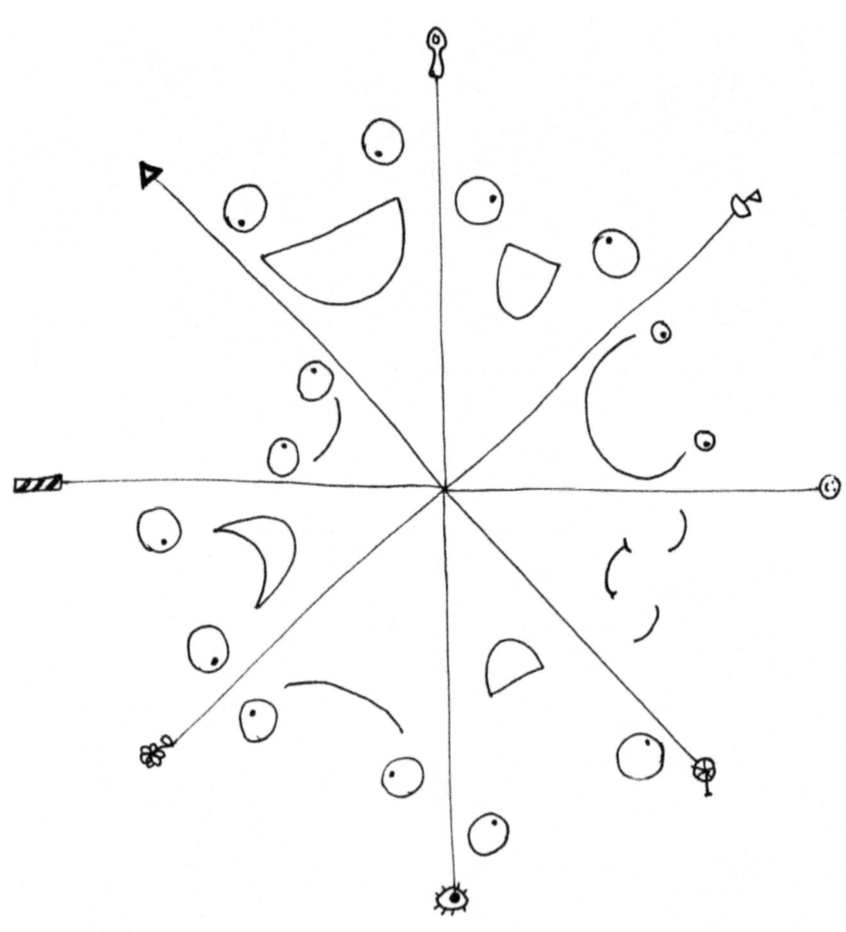

What would you like your balance of Love
and Fear to look like?

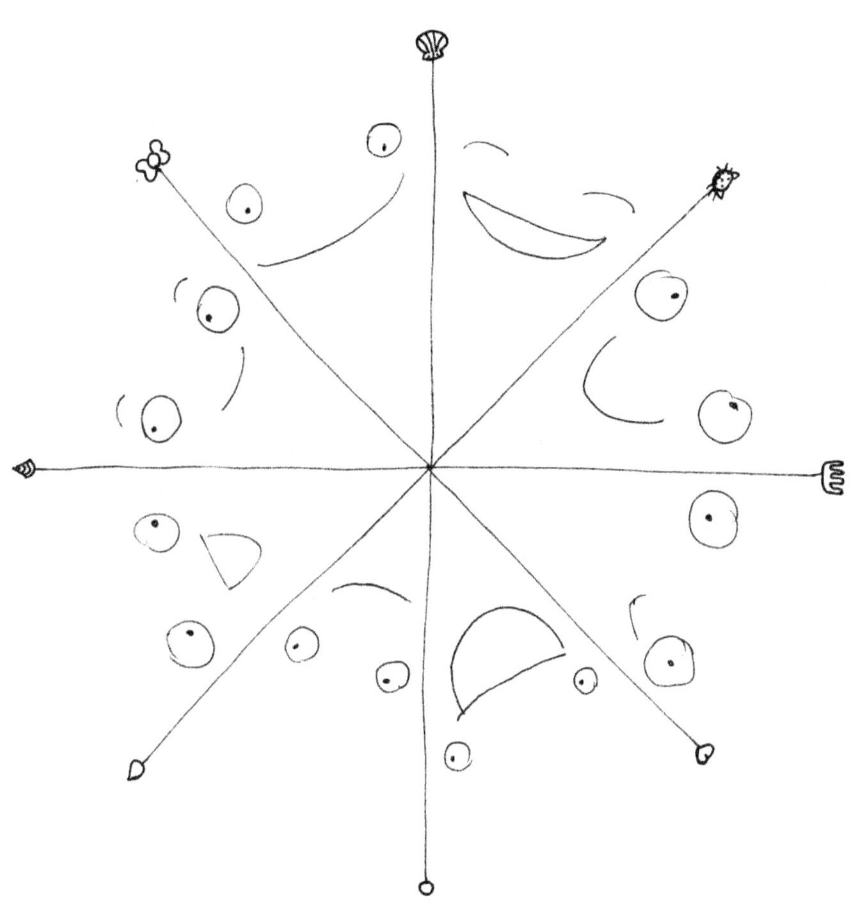

75

Now let's look at our Health, Family/
Friends, Work, and Spirit/Philosophy Pieces.
How much time do you feel like you spend
focusing on each of these areas?

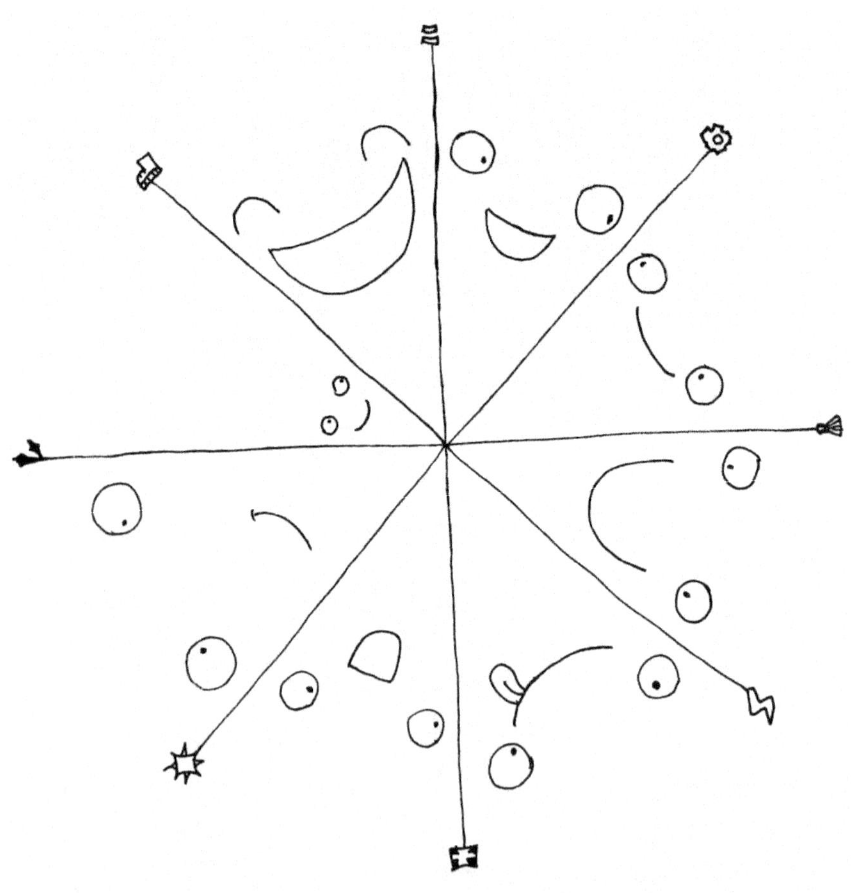

What would you like your balance to look like?

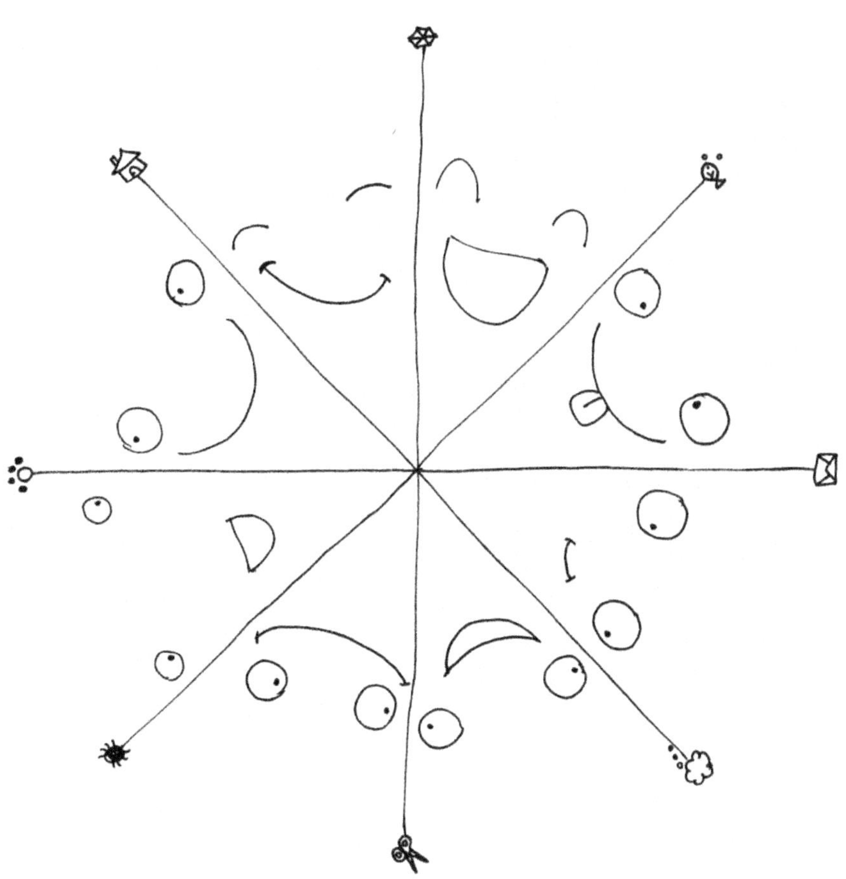

It's good to believe in things that are meant to be. Time does not bind these things. This book represents an idea that needed to be born, time and thought to grow, and a creative partnership to make it come alive. I hope you are inspired by the journey and premise of this book.

May your pies be perfect!

-Mark